Stuff Every

# DAD

Should Know

Library of Congress Cataloging in Publication Number: 2011933430

ISBN: 978-1-59474-553-9

Printed in China

Typeset in Goudy and Monotype Old Style

Designed by Katie Hatz
Illustrations by Kate Francis
Production management by John J. McGurk

10 9 8 7 6 5 4 3 2

Quirk Books
215 Church Street
Philadelphia, PA 19106
quirkbooks.com

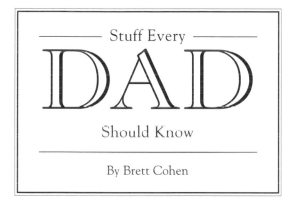

Stuff Every

# DAD

Should Know

By Brett Cohen

QUIRK BOOKS

PHILADELPHIA

*To my children, Ilivia and Sawyer,*
*and to my wife, Randi*

## Introduction

Welcome to fatherhood! You've coached Mom through labor, cut the umbilical cord, and passed out the cigars. You've brought home your bundle of joy. And then it hits you: Now what?

Sure, the adventures of New Dad sound an awful lot like the adventures of Bachelor Man:

- Late nights with a bottle in your hand
- Working extra hard to get her into bed
- Explaining why it's OK for you to spend some time apart
- Sleepover parties with tons of girls
- Talking about drugs and alcohol

But now all these activities have a whole new spin. That late-night bottle is full of baby formula, not Sam Adams. You're luring that cutie-pie to bed by reading a story, clearing the room of monsters, and fetching "one last glass of water" before retreating to the blissful haven of your own room. That talk about spending time apart is going to happen while your child wails in despair as you try to say good-bye and drive away on the first day of school. The sleepover party—yeah, your job is to rent a movie that a roomful of nine-year-olds will all like. And talking about mood-altering substances gets a lot less funny and a lot more serious when you're the one explaining to your child why she should not use them.

It's a whole new world, huh? Have no fear. This book is jam-packed with information and resources to help you along the way.

Always remember: Being a dad is life altering—for the better. You will marvel at your child's first step and cheer at the first soccer game. You will laugh your pants off watching your child's first meal and, decades later, cry your eyes out at the wedding rehearsal dinner.

A lifetime of joy awaits. Also, a lifetime of stuff that needs doing. Fortunately, what you are holding is *Stuff Every Dad Should Know*.

Baby Stuff

## How to Start Saving for College

Surprise! You thought we were going to start with something about infant care, didn't you? Welcome to your new life. For the next two decades, starting today if not sooner, you will be locking away a piece of your income every week to help ensure that your kid has as many options as possible come graduation day.

- **Start small and start now.** Take a look at your budget and allocate whatever you can. Can you find $1 per day to put aside? $2 per day? Start there. Just by opening the account and contributing monthly, you'll have taken a huge step toward your goal.

- **Increase your investment over time.** Assess your contribution annually. Increase it commensurately to any rise in your income. Anytime you're fortunate enough to get a bonus, a portion should be deposited into the college account. And any total-surprise windfalls, like winnings from your fantasy football league, should go straight into the account.

- **Speak to a financial advisor.** Around your child's fifth birthday, seek advice on ways to help grow the college fund even more quickly. An advisor can point you to 529 savings plans, mutual funds, stocks, and bonds.

## How to Hold Your Baby

OK, *now* we come to the infant-care part. Holding and comforting your child is the most basic form of bonding. So let's start off right.

1. Slide one hand under your baby's neck and head. Remember to always support a baby's head and neck, especially at the newborn stage.

2. Slide the other hand under your baby's bottom and back.

3. Lift your baby up and bring him close to your body.

4. From this position, you can raise your baby so his head rests on the front of your shoulder. Continue to support his bottom with your other hand.

5. Alternately, you can guide your baby's head and neck into the crook of your arm to cradle him. For added support, tuck your other arm under him as well.

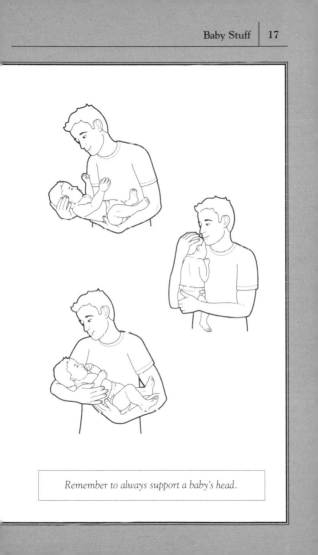

*Remember to always support a baby's head.*

## How to Change a Diaper

It's been said that the first time is the hardest. This is true. It's usually not pretty in there, but you'll get used to it quickly. So man up, rip off the tabs, and follow these instructions to get in and out as efficiently as possible.

1. Gather all the items you need: child, fresh diaper, baby wipes.

2. Lay your baby faceup on either a changing table or a changing pad arranged on the floor. If using a changing table, make certain to fasten the safety straps. I prefer a changing pad on the floor because it's safer and easier to position yourself in front of the baby.

3. Place the fresh, open diaper under your baby's still-dirty-diapered bottom with the tabs on the portion that is under the baby's bottom. Doing this now provides an additional layer between the mess and whatever surface you're using, which is important since it will need to be cleaned at the end.

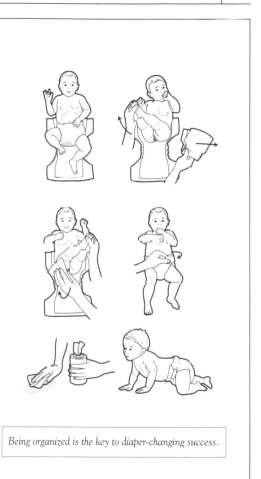

*Being organized is the key to diaper-changing success.*

4. Unfasten the diaper tabs and use one hand to lift your baby's ankles so that her bottom is raised slightly above the dirty diaper. You may want to strategically place a baby wipe to avoid being sprayed by an accidental urination.

5. Clean the messy area with baby wipes. Always wipe from front to back, especially when wiping a baby girl.

6. Once clean, apply lotions or ointments recommended by your doctor.

7. Close the diaper by folding up the front section and opening and securing the sticky tabs. Do not make the diaper too tight or leave it too loose. You should be able to slide one or two fingers between the belly and the diaper.

8. Dispose of the messy diaper and wipes in a diaper pail.

9. Wash your hands and the changing area.

# How to Give Your Baby a Bath

You should give your baby a bath about three times per week. Here's what to expect: He'll probably cry. He'll almost surely squirm. And you'll both end up pretty wet. Enjoy!

1. In the early days, until the umbilical cord falls off, you should give your baby only a sponge bath. After the cord falls off, you can clean your baby in a small plastic bathtub or a sink.

2. Gather all the items you'll need for bathing, including a soap approved for use on babies, baby shampoo, a soft washcloth, and a fluffy towel.

3. Fill the tub or sink with two to three inches of warm (not hot) water.

4. Undress your baby.

5. Place your baby in the tub or sink. You will need to support the baby's back and neck throughout the bath unless you're using a specially designed baby tub that properly props up your child's body.

6. Use the washcloth to wet your baby's head. Squeeze a small dollop of baby shampoo and gently lather his head. Rinse the washcloth and squeeze water over his head to wash away the shampoo. Be careful to avoid getting any suds in his eyes.

7. Using the washcloth and soap (sparingly), wash your baby's body. When finished, use a rinsed washcloth to wipe away the soap.

8. Remove your baby from the tub and wrap him in a dry towel. Gently pat him all over to make sure he's completely dry.

**Caution:** Never leave your baby alone in the tub or sink.

## How to Feed Your Baby from a Bottle

Got formula? Unless the child's mother is breast-feeding, you'd better have some on hand. It's what's for dinner! Baby formula might seem "less filling" to you, but don't worry—your child will probably find that it "tastes great." Here's how you make sure it's well received.

1. Prepare the formula according to the package directions. Let's repeat that: *Read the directions*. Not all formulas are identical.

2. If you'd like to bring the bottle to room temperature, run it under warm water for a minute or two. Do *not* heat the bottle in the microwave.

3. Sit down. Position your baby in the cradle position with his head in the crook of your arm and raised slightly above the rest of his body. For comfort, you may want to rest your arm or your baby's bottom on your lap.

4. Fasten a bib around the baby's neck to prevent soiling or wetting his clothing.

5. Place the bottle upside down or in a position that fills the nipple with formula.

6. Gently position the nipple inside your baby's mouth. His reflex should kick in, and he will start sucking.

7. Remove the bottle after five or ten minutes or if feeding has stalled.

8. Burp your baby. (See page 26.)

9. Continue feeding until the baby is full or the bottle is empty. Each baby will eat a different amount; there's no true standard. However, if you think your baby isn't eating enough, consult your pediatrician.

# What If Mom Is Breast-feeding?

Congratulations—that means *your* nipples get to relax and take it easy! Just kidding. But when Mom breast-feeds, it's common for Dad to feel left out, as though you're unable to bond with your baby in the same way. That doesn't have to be the case. It's important to remember that breast-feeding is difficult; your partner may struggle with it and find it extremely stressful. You can help ease this stress by supporting her and reinforcing her decision. You can let her see right from the start that you're there at her side by getting up together when the baby wakes during the night. You may not be able to breast-feed, but you can certainly be the one to change the baby's diaper and bring the child to Mom. And once your baby has taken to the breast milk and your partner is expressing her milk into a bottle, then you, too, can feed the baby as needed.

## How to Burp Your Baby

There's an art to burping a baby—one that doesn't involve belching out the ABCs, that is. Here are two basic styles.

1. Drape a burp cloth, bib, or towel over your shoulder.

2. Rest your baby's head on the cloth-covered shoulder so that her chest lies against your chest. Support her bottom with that same arm.

3. Rub her back by making small circles between her shoulder blades.

4. If your baby doesn't burp after five minutes, you should gently pat her on the back, starting near her bottom and working your way up toward her shoulders.

5. If after another five minutes she still doesn't burp, you can continue feeding.

6. Alternately, you could position the baby on your lap, in a sitting position, with her face out and her body leaning forward slightly. Then follow steps 3–5 as above.

## How to Get Some Sleep When Your Baby Won't

Few babies younger than four months will sleep through the night; many won't do so until they're a year old. But don't panic. That doesn't mean that you, too, have to go sleepless, though it may occasionally feel that way. Here are two methods to help you string together enough Zs to make it through the many weeks of round-the-clock feedings.

- **Alternate feedings with your partner.** Feed the baby around 8 p.m. Send Mom to bed around 9 p.m. while you stay awake for the 11 p.m. feeding. Mom gets up for the 2 a.m. feeding while you sleep blissfully. Toss a coin to see who gets the 5 a.m. feeding. Either way, you each nab a solid 5 to 6 hours of rest, plus a few bonus hours to boot.

- **Alternate nights with your partner.** Although not an ideal situation for every couple, some would rather be on duty for an entire night, with one ear at attention all night, and then off duty and sleeping peacefully the next.

## Five Tips for Caring for Your Wife or Partner

- **Be supportive.** A new baby can sometimes be overwhelming; you and your partner will have moments when you doubt your parenting skills, decisions, and sanity. Don't let her fall prey to the second-guessing—assure her frequently and sincerely that she's being a great mother.

- **Be a hands-on dad.** This book introduces you to the basic skills to help bathe, diaper, feed, and burp your baby. Do these things. Your relationships with your children and their mother will be all the stronger thanks to your daily participation in the parenting trenches.

- **Let her sleep.** Sleep deprivation can cause a lot of anxiety, and anxiety can strain your relationship. Relieve Mom of duty at every possible opportunity so she can close her eyes and recoup.

- **Don't let her hunker down.** After a new baby is born, Dad will often be the first to go back to a regular work schedule, leaving

Mom to mind the home front. That means she's on the clock 24 hours a day. Not only can such constant responsibility become mind-numbing, it can be extremely stressful as well. Whenever possible, kick her out of the house for a much-needed break. Encourage her to get a manicure or go to the gym or meet a friend for coffee. She'll come back recharged and refreshed.

- **Bask in the glow.** When things settle down for a moment, remind her about how great this whole family thing is. The sleepless nights will pass. So, too, will the constant self-doubt. Remind yourselves of that hopefully-not-so-distant future, and enjoy your baby in that moment.

## How to Introduce Solid Food

When your baby is between the ages of 4 and 6 months, you can start to introduce solid food. Unfortunately, that doesn't mean you can ditch the bottle feedings. You'll need to provide a mix of solid food and formula (or breast milk) until the baby reaches the year mark. Here are some tips to transition from bottle-feeding to solid food and beyond.

1. Baby rice cereal makes an ideal transition to solid food because it is bland, has a liquid base, and is typically less allergenic than most foods. Be sure to follow the preparation instructions on the package.

2. Start by feeding your baby as you normally do, that is, using a bottle or breast-feeding.

3. Using a soft-tipped spoon, feed him a small amount—just a fingertip's worth—of the rice cereal mixture. If he's reluctant to taste it, be patient.

4. In the beginning, feed your baby rice cereal only once per day; this is just practice and should not be viewed as a true

meal. As he eats more of the rice cereal, it can then take the place of one of the daily bottle feedings.

5. After your baby grows more accustomed to eating solid food, you can introduce strained or mashed fruits and vegetables. These are typical baby foods you can find in a store.

6. Between 10 and 12 months, your baby may be ready for chopped table foods. Remember to continue to alternate formula or breast-feedings with his meals.

## Foods to Avoid

In general, the following foods should be avoided until your child is one year old. And, even then, you should pay close attention to your child's reaction to them.

### Foods with allergy potential

- Honey
- Peanuts and peanut-based products (peanut butter, foods cooked in peanut oil, etc.)
- Juice
- Whole cow's milk

### Foods that can cause digestive problems

- Citrus fruits and juices
- Caffeine
- Egg whites

## Foods that are notorious for being a choking hazard

- Large chunks of food (Vegetables, such as carrots and green beans, should be cooked until they're soft and then sliced and diced into manageable bite size. Fruits, like grapes and melon, should be cut into smaller pieces.)

- Small hard foods, like popcorn and raisins

- Chewy foods, like marshmallows and gummy bears

## Baby Clothes Dos and Don'ts

Nowadays, baby clothes are a mix of fashion and function. We'll discuss functionality here and leave the fashion decisions to you.

- **Consider your baby's size.** Lucky for you, most baby clothes are tagged by age. So, a tag might say "newborn," "0–3 months," "3–6 months," etc., up to "24 months." Then it moves into toddler sizes based on age. So "2T" is meant for a two-year-old toddler. Unless your child is substantially bigger than average, it's pretty easy to identify the appropriate sizes.

- **Consider the weather.** Dressing your baby in layers will allow her to stay warm and cool off when necessary. Choose clothing that's easy to remove.

- **Consider the messy diaper.** Yet another reason to opt for easily removable clothing. Also, keep in mind that a full diaper has the potential for disaster; layering a onesie over a diaper and under clothes will help protect clothes against leakage.

- **Consider the mess.** Every baby is going to spit up and spill things, and there's always the chance of diaper mishaps. Hence the really strong argument for function over fashion. Don't spend a ton of money on baby clothes, because not only will your baby quickly grow out of them, she'll probably also stain the heck out of them along the way.

- **Consider your baby's gender.** Whether you choose to dress your boy in pink and your girl in blue is up to you. Just keep in mind that, for good or ill, color coding is an easy way to let the rest of the world know what pronoun to use without having to ask. (Dresses and hair bands also accomplish this point.)

## How to Manage the Grandparents

Most grandparents want to help—and many usually have the experience to do so. You must determine for yourself when the help edges over the line and becomes a nuisance. Here are some tips to foster a healthy intergenerational relationship.

- **Maintain an open dialogue.** Your partner may want her mom around all the time, especially in the early days. You may want your mom around, too. Maybe one or both are too overbearing and tend to add more stress to the situation. Reach an understanding with your wife that works for you both. Then communicate that plan, diplomatically and authoritatively, to both sets of grandparents.

- **Set a schedule.** If the grandparents live close by, set up regular or semiregular times for them to stop over to play or babysit. These can be great opportunities for you and your wife to spend a bit of time together—and alone.

- **Invite them along.** Activities away from the home are perfect occasions to invite the grandparents. Family road trip to the zoo!

- **Set up boundaries.** Grandparents tend to live by their own set of rules. And, frankly, they've probably earned it. But time with the grandparents shouldn't mean that all your hard work flies out the window. Ask them to abide by and enforce the rules and schedule for your child that you have carefully set in place.

- **That said, allow them to indulge.** A relationship with a grandparent should be fun. Breaking the rules every now and then is OK.

## Essential Items in a Daddy Diaper Bag

It's inevitable. You will be alone with your child and, for some reason or another, you'll have to leave the house. Hopefully, your wife has selected a unisex diaper bag so that you don't feel self-conscious about carrying a "man purse." Either way, you may want to consider purchasing your own handy carryall, something more dad specific, that lets you confidently approach all situations as the ultimate well-prepared scout. Essential items include the following.

- Age-appropriate formula and bottle, food, spoon, snack cup, sippy cup
- Bib and burp cloth
- Diapers, changing pad, baby wipes, diaper baggies
- Pacifier
- Extra set of clothes
- Toys
- Dad items: camera, cell phone, wallet

*"It's called a satchel. Indiana Jones wears one."*
—Alan Garner, The Hangover

## Male Humor: What Is and Is Not Funny

If we can't find the comedy in rearing children, we're doomed. But let's face it: men and women frequently have different senses of humor. Jokes are supposed to relieve life's tension, not make it worse, so keep these things in mind when cracking wise about your baby.

- **Safety always comes first.** It should go without saying, but dangling your baby over a railing is not safe and not funny.

- **Harmless silliness makes for a good photo.** Putting your sunglasses on the baby is funny—and can be immortalized in a picture.

- **Bathroom humor is a given.** Always funny. And pretty much expected.

- **Smart dads are self-deprecating.** When the baby pees on you while you're changing the diaper, it's funny. When he pees on your wife, it's not funny . . . unless she laughs first.

## Five Great Songs to Sing to Your Baby

Singing is a great way to comfort, or energize, your baby, depending on the setting. Here's a quick refresher on some of the standards.

### Twinkle, Twinkle, Little Star

Use this favorite at bedtime to rock your baby to sleep.

> *Twinkle, twinkle, little star*
> *How I wonder what you are*
> *Up above the world so high*
> *Like a diamond in the sky*
> *Twinkle, twinkle, little star*
> *How I wonder what you are*

### The Itsy-Bitsy Spider

This is a great playtime song. Be sure to learn the hand gestures that go along with the words.

> *The Itsy-Bitsy Spider climbed up the water*
> *    spout,*
> *Down came the rain and washed the spider out.*

*Out came the sun and dried up all the rain,*
*And the Itsy-Bitsy Spider climbed up the*
*spout again.*

### Row, Row, Row Your Boat

Try this one while sitting on the ground facing
your baby. Hold hands and rock to and fro as if
you're rowing a boat together.

*Row, row, row your boat,*
*Gently down the stream.*
*Merrily, merrily, merrily, merrily,*
*Life is but a dream.*
*Rock, rock, rock your boat,*
*Gently down the stream.*
*If you see a crocodile,*
*Don't forget to SCREAM!*

### Old MacDonald Had a Farm

This ditty is a great way to help your child learn
animals and the sounds they make.

*Old MacDonald had a farm,*
*E-I-E-I-O*
*And on his farm he had a pig.*

*E-I-E-I-O*
*With an oink-oink here and an oink-oink there*
*Here an oink, there an oink, everywhere*
    *an oink-oink*
*Old MacDonald had a farm,*
*E-I-E-I-O*

(Repeat with whatever animal you'd like.)

### Five Little Monkeys

Here's a fun song for older children to sing along with.

*Five little monkeys jumping on the bed,*
*One fell off and bumped his head.*
*Mama called the doctor and the doctor said,*
*"No more monkeys jumping on the bed!"*
*Four little monkeys jumping on the bed,*
*One fell off and bumped his head.*
*Mama called the doctor and the doctor said,*
*"No more monkeys jumping on the bed!"*

(Repeat with three, two, one, and no more monkeys.)

# Little Kid
# Stuff

## How to Get Your Child to Eat

As your child grows, he will begin to exert his will a little bit. Although it's not quite teenage rebellion, he'll want to make his own decisions. As a baby becomes a toddler, mealtime is one area that can frustrate new and seasoned parents alike. It may mean simply a change in what foods your child wants or a downright refusal to eat altogether. Try these tips and tactics to smooth over sit-downs at the family table.

- **Offer a selection.** Let your child select something meal related, whether the plate or his seat at the table or even the food that's served. He may be more likely to eat if he feels empowered, having taken part in the decision-making process.

- **Include him in the preparation.** Ask your child if he wants to taste the meal as you make it, so he knows it tastes good. Or ask him to help set the table, so he feels part of the entire meal-making routine.

- **Get creative.** Use a cookie cutter to cut sandwiches into kid-friendly shapes. Give the food funny names. Arrange items on his plate in the shape of a smiley face. Have fun with food, and your child will likely follow suit.

- **Insert entertainment.** Invite a stuffed animal to join you for lunch. Or read a book, taking a bite after each page.

- **Remember that he won't really starve.** So pick your battles—sometimes kids just won't eat. If your child refuses food at mealtime, offer him something later. If, however, he skips several meals and shows no interest in eating or snacking, then consult your pediatrician.

## How to Make a Peanut Butter and Jelly Sandwich

Sounds simple, right? And yet whipping up this simplest of everyday go-to lunches has details you may not have considered. Here are the PB&J basics every dad should know!

1. Grab two slices of bread (white is a favorite, but whole wheat is healthier), peanut butter, and jelly. Creamy varieties are favored by most little kids. And though grape jelly is the reliable all-American standard, don't be shy about stocking several different kinds to introduce your child to new tastes.

2. Put an apron on yourself and a pint-size one on your child, too. Not only will it protect her clothing, but it will increase her feeling of involvement.

3. Using a butter knife, spread the peanut butter on one side of a piece of bread. Cover it evenly, but don't overdo it. You're buttering bread, not icing a cake.

4. Dollop a spoonful of jelly onto one side of the other piece of bread. Spread it evenly on the bread.

5. Teach your child about the construction of a sandwich, picking up the bread by the dry undersides and pressing them together to keep the messy stuff in the middle.

6. If your child wants you to cut the crusts off the sandwich, go ahead and do it. You're probably hungry anyway, so become the Crust Monster.

7. You can slice the sandwich into traditional halves (down the middle or on the diagonal) or quarters or use a large cookie cutter to cut out unusual shapes. Allow your child to press the cookie cutter into the sandwich, assisting as necessary. Guaranteed to make any kid, big or small, smile.

## Fifteen Tips for Childproofing Your House

Children are curious creatures. And curious creatures like to touch things. Touching things that shouldn't be touched can be dangerous. Therefore, eliminate danger as best you can from your home.

- Get down on all fours and crawl around your entire home. Yes, really. Doing so will allow you to see things from your baby's perspective and understand firsthand what he can see and reach. Anything dangerous in your path should be assessed and addressed. The same goes for any object you consider too valuable to break—it's time to move that collection of vintage records to a higher shelf.

- Examine the area around your baby's crib, not just for items that are inherently dangerous, but also for things that could inspire your child to reach for them and fall. Consider wall fixtures, blankets, toys, stuffed animals, and the like.

- Use childproof locks to secure kitchen cupboards and drawers. The locks will deter most children. Move all knives and cleaning solutions to higher (locked) cabinets.

- Secure all electrical sockets with child-proof plugs or covers.

- Apply foam rubber bumpers to sharp edges and corners of coffee tables, end tables, and fireplaces.

- Secure all high-standing furniture to a wall, including bookshelves, entertainment units, large televisions, and dressers and chests of drawers. If a child can climb on it, there's a good chance he can pull it onto himself, causing serious injury. Similarly, do not place heavy items near the edges of shelves or tables.

- Install gates at the top and bottom of all stairs.

- Install child locks on doors leading to rooms you don't want your child to enter without your permission or oversight, for instance, the basement, office, garage, utility room (containing a hot water heater and/or furnace), closet, and pantry.

- Take note of plants that may be in the child's reach. Many houseplants are poisonous or can be hazardous if consumed or touched.

- Watch for smaller items that may present a choking hazard, including refrigerator magnets, jewelry, and older children's toys.

- Secure the hanging strings from window blinds out of the children's reach, for they may cause strangulation.

- Install a carbon monoxide detector and smoke alarm in your child's room.

- Be concerned about water. Although most accidents occur in the bathroom, a child can drown in a surprisingly small amount of water. Even the location of a dog's water bowl should be considered. Install toilet seat locks. And, of course, safeguard a swimming pool by installing a fence and a lock that's out of children's reach.

- Consider hiring a professional. It may seem like an easy job and an unnecessary expense, but the safety of your child is at stake. Indeed, this job might be one for which you should spring for an expert and buy yourself some peace of mind. Priceless.

- And, lastly, always keep an eye on your child. Even with all these precautions, there is no replacement for a watchful parent.

## Elements of a First-Aid Kit

You've probably already got a tool kit, but this is your *other* tool kit. Every home in which a child lives needs a first-aid kit. Fortunately, they are easy to assemble and include nothing as expensive as a power drill.

- Infant and/or child thermometer(s): digital, ear, and rectal
- Rubbing-alcohol swabs (to clean the thermometer)
- Petroleum jelly (to lubricate the rectal thermometer)
- Infants' or Children's Tylenol or ibuprofen, used to relieve fevers, as recommended by your pediatrician
- Saline nose drops to clear a stuffy nose
- Nasal aspirator
- Topical calamine lotion to relieve insect bites and itchy rashes
- Antibiotic ointment for cuts and bruises
- Adhesive bandages for cuts and bruises (These days bandages come with boo-boo-healing

cartoon characters printed on them.)

- Gauze roll, gauze pads, and adhesive tape for larger cuts and bruises
- Tweezers and scissors

Note: Because of its contents, be sure to store the first-aid kit out of your child's reach.

## How to Fix a Boo-Boo

If you've followed our advice on page 54 and prepared a proper first-aid kit, good job! There should now be no crisis when addressing a minor bump or bruise. In fact, doing so will likely be more about calming your child than soothing the injury.

1. Start by administering the appropriate amount of hugs and kisses. (For the sorts of boo-boos that basically amount to "I fell down and banged myself, and it startled me," a long hug and a kiss to the affected area will sometimes be enough to squelch the sniffles.)

2. If your child has a scrape or small cut, rinse it thoroughly using a clean washcloth, soap, and warm running water.

3. If dirt particles or (heaven forbid!) splinters stubbornly linger in the wound, clean a pair of tweezers with rubbing alcohol and use them to gently remove the debris.

4. Apply a small amount of antibiotic ointment to the clean cut.

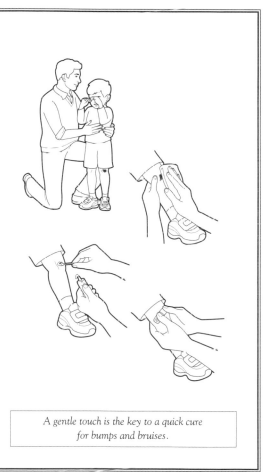

*A gentle touch is the key to a quick cure*
*for bumps and bruises.*

5. If the cut is small enough, simply place an adhesive bandage over it. For scrapes covering a slightly larger surface, such as brush burns, use a gauze pad and adhesive wrap.

6. Give it another kiss.

## Tips and Tricks for Child Hygiene

Bathing? Getting clean? To a kid, this sounds like a terrible chore. But, fortunately, children love games, and when they're young you can convince them that almost *anything* is a game. So before your child has a chance to form a contrary attitude toward scrubbing, start the sanitary routine on a playful note.

### Bath Time

- **Offer variety.** Offer your child his choice of washcloth, or ask whether he wants a bubble bath or a suds-less soak in the regular tub.

- **Include your child in bath prep.** Teach him how to turn on the water, reminding him to do so only when you are in the room. Or, while you fill the tub, have him gather a few waterproof toys to bring into the bath.

- **Get creative.** Add a drop of food dye to bathwater to change its color. Or play music and sing a "washing song."

### Brushing Teeth

- **Offer a selection.** While at the store, let your child pick out her own toothbrush and special flavor of toothpaste. Kid-themed novelty toothbrushes are great. Don't underestimate the excitement children can whip up at the prospect of their favorite cartoon character exploring their mouths!

- **Get creative.** Use puppets to hold the toothbrush. Give the toothbrush a silly name. Or have a contest to see who can brush their teeth the longest. Sneaky!

- **Let her watch you brush.** Make a big spectacle about how good it feels when you brush your own teeth. Set a good example and your children will follow suit.

### Brushing Hair

- **Get the facts.** Research your child's hair type; different textures and lengths may require special treatment and brushes. Opt for a no-tangle spray to prevent knots that cause pain when pulled during brushing.

- **Use distractions.** Comb your child's hair while he's still playing in the bath or enjoying a quiet postbath activity, like reading a book.

- **Be creative.** Pretend to brush his favorite toy's hair, or let him brush it. Hey, if Optimus Prime or Winnie the Pooh does it, it must be fun, right?

## Five Great Books to Read to Your Child

Reading is one of the fundamentals of life. Reading to your child at an early age fosters the imagination and cultivates an appreciation for books and a love for stories. On top of all that, reading a book together before bedtime establishes a nightly ritual that allows you and your child to wind down and share a quiet moment at the end of the day. The following are some favorite classics that stimulate a young child's sense of wonder.

- ***The Very Hungry Caterpillar* by Eric Carle.** An easy read that will teach your child the days of the week as well as how to count along as the caterpillar eats its way through a variety of tasty treats.

- ***Harold and the Purple Crayon* by Crockett Johnson.** Resourceful young Harold uses his imagination—and, of course, a violet-hued drawing implement—to create a magical world where he can go adventuring, bringing your child along for the ride.

- **Where the Wild Things Are by Maurice Sendak.** When Max is sent to his room without any supper, he dreams up a land where he is king of all the wild beasts. Max has fun, but along the way he learns some valuable life lessons about responsibility, love, and family.

- **Diary of a Wombat by Jackie French.** A funny story about the simple daily life of a wombat, which changes considerably when the wombat meets her new human neighbors. Your child will laugh as the wombat trains her adoptive family to feed her carrots.

- **Green Eggs and Ham by Dr. Seuss.** How do we choose just one Dr. Seuss book? Well, in this all-time classic, the joyfully silly rhymes and iconic illustrations combine to tell the story of Sam, who learns to love his green eggs and ham. Both you and your child will appreciate the tongue-twisting narration.

## How to Teach Your Child to Share

Babies are rightfully made to feel like the center of our universe. Yet, when they become toddlers, we expect them to grasp the idea that other people matter, too. Hence the concept of sharing. For some, it comes easy. For others, it's a foreign concept that needs to be taught and reinforced.

- **Set a good example.** Children model their behavior on yours, whether good or bad. Show what it means to share when you give her your own things, and encourage her to do the same.

- **Use whatever language works.** Introduce a variety of related words and concepts, like "trading" and "taking turns." Ask her to trade one toy with a friend, or give her a turn with the toy and then let the friend have a turn.

- **Heap on the praise.** When she shares, applaud and approve to reinforce good behavior.

- **Be respectful of her wishes.** If she's unwilling to share, be mindful of her reasons. Are the other children mishandling her toy in a way that upsets her? Or are there a few special toys she particularly adores, and perhaps those items should be put away before a play-date? There's nothing wrong with keeping a few precious objects just for her.

## How to Rid a Room of Monsters

When an invisible beast is hiding in your children's room, who they gonna call? That's right: you. You are now ghostbuster in chief. The key to ridding a room of monsters is to find just the right blend of comedy and creativity. Of course, you know the monster isn't real, but in the middle of the night your child isn't looking to be reasoned with. So get imaginative and play along. Here are a few ideas.

- **Perform a thorough search.** Follow your child's lead, since he's the one who's been pondering the likeliest monster hiding spots. Use a flashlight to search under the bed, inside the closet, and behind the furniture. See, no monsters!

- **Make up a story.** Tell your child that only nice monsters live in your house, and their names are George and Kitty.

- **Mix up a monster-repellant spray.** Solicit your child's help in gathering ingredients, such as water and a variety of

*Turn scary monsters into friends with a good story.*

spices. Pour them into a spray bottle. Walk around the room, spritzing under the bed, inside the closet, and behind the furniture.

- **Introduce a guardian.** Offer him a new stuffed animal, doll, or toy that has been empowered to protect children from monsters. If he's still unconvinced, heap on the hype. Explain that this protector has been passed through three generations of children who all grew up safe and sound.

## How to Squelch a Temper Tantrum

Remember that poor SOB at the mall whose kid was freaking out? Remember how you said that would never happen to you? Well, guess what: It's probably going to happen to you. Children like to test their control and assert their will, but often they don't yet have the maturity to properly express themselves. Hence, a tantrum. When it happens, stay calm and try some of these techniques.

- **Identify the source.** Take a moment to understand why your child is having a tantrum. Knowing this information may suggest a solution or, at the very least, help you prevent a future recurrence. (For instance, if he freaks out every time it's time to leave, make sure you give him advance notice next time.)

- **Ignore the outburst.** As long as your child isn't putting himself or someone else in danger, try simply going about your business. If his tactic to get attention doesn't work, he may calm down on his own.

- **Remove the child from the situation.** A quick trip to the bathroom or into a hallway will change the setting and, perhaps, change the mood.

- **Remind your child to express himself.** Try to quiet him and then ask why he's so upset. Get him to talk through his feelings, instead of yelling.

- **Stand your ground.** Never, ever give in to the demands of a tantrum. Doing so only reinforces bad behavior and ensures that it will happen again.

## How to Say "No"

As your child grows out of babyhood and into kidhood, you'll find yourself needing to engage in more discipline and danger prevention. This is a natural process as children test their boundaries, try new things, and indulge their curiosities. No one likes to hear, or say, "no," but it's a giant part of your job as a parent—and it's important to do it well.

- **Be firm.** When you say "no," mean it and do not relent. Be consistent in your tone and body language. (Oftentimes, you can substitute a look that sends the same message as the word.)

- **Offer an alternative.** Make sure you aren't *only* saying "no." Your child needs to know that you do want her to do things, just not *that* thing. So try including alternatives: "You may not throw the ball in the house, but you may race trucks across the floor."

- **Consider the situation.** It's unrealistic to expect a child to sit still all day while you do grown-up things. If you find she's getting into too much trouble around the house, take her outside and let her run around for a while. Indulge her curiosities with lots of "yes" reinforcement.

## How to Potty-Train Your Child

Leaving behind diapers for the potty is a big event for your child—and you. You finally get to take a huge step away from that diaper bag. It's a long process, though, and it requires tons of reinforcement. The ingredients for a successful training session are simple: a potty chair, lots of liquids (water, juice), lots of water-based fruits (watermelon), stickers, and a new pair of underwear (with your child's favorite character printed on it). Here's how to begin.

1. Set aside a full day. If the weather permits, plan to spend it in the backyard.

2. Dress your child in a dress (girls) or long T-shirt (boys or girls). No diaper or pants.

3. Show the underwear, and use it as a motivating force. Explain that today your child is going to practice going on the potty and that when she goes on the potty, she'll be able to wear big-kid underwear like *this*. (Proudly display aforementioned underwear bearing much-loved cartoon character.)

4. Start feeding her the fruit and lots of liquids. Continuing playing.

5. Have her sit on the potty chair every 30 minutes. Let her stay there for a minute or two. If she goes, heap on tons of praise. Give her a sticker. If she doesn't go, let her go back to playing.

6. Children will naturally have an accident or two during this process. Encourage her to control the urge to go and run over to the potty chair. Praise her each time she goes successfully and give her a sticker.

7. Repeat this process all day long.

8. By the end of the day, your child should have the routine down pat and will be heading to the potty on her own terms.

9. Continue the reinforcement for a week or two. And be prepared for accidents—they're going to happen. So don't scold, and practice patience.

## Tips and Tricks for Managing Sibling Relations

So you survived the first child and went back for another? Congrats! By this point, you probably know that raising two children is more than twice as hard as raising one. You'll be faced with a whole new set of parenting challenges—not just logistical organization, but interpersonal dynamics. These include that oldest human conflict of them all: sibling rivalry. It's difficult to prevent but can be managed properly with a bit of sensitivity.

- **Be fair, but be rational.** Ensuring that everyone gets equal attention is fair. Ensuring that everyone gets equal attention on one child's birthday is irrational. Children need to feel special sometimes. Dole out the specialness in equal increments, but spread it out over time.

- **Don't rush to judgment.** If a fight or argument breaks out, don't assume you know the whole story. Take a moment to find out what led up to the incident to ensure you're properly assessing the situation.

- **Develop a system.** Identify which activities lead to the biggest rivalry: pushing the elevator button, choosing a TV show, etc. Set up a schedule for alternating whose turn it is to do what.

- **Create a mutual goal.** If the rivalry gets unbearable, introduce a reward based on good behavior from all parties. If they both behave until dinner, then they both get a special dessert.

- **Heap on praise.** Note the times your children do get along well. Praise and reward this behavior.

## How to Photograph Your Child

Kids are a constantly moving blur of activity. That isn't exactly the ideal subject for a photograph . . . or is it? Here's the thing: You don't need to take idyllic portraits of your perfectly poised children; that's a job for the professionals. Your job is to take a mellow approach to snapping those true, candid moments that tell the real story of your child.

- **There's no such thing as the perfect shot.** So don't wait for it. Throwing his hands in the air, chewing on a block in her mouth, smashing birthday cake on his brother's face—these aren't the scenes to avoid, they're the moments to capture.

- **Tell a story.** Set up a scene and let your child come to it. If she's into cooking, invite her to bake a cake with you. If he's into LEGOs, ask him to build you a house. Then snap away as your child does what comes naturally.

- **Remember the basics.** Use a flash when needed. Many cameras now come with a "pets and children" setting that reduces the blur of a moving subject.

- **Experiment.** Mix close-ups with wider shots. Take pictures from above and below. Don't be afraid of too-bright days or pitch-black nights. With the ease and affordability of digital cameras, deleting poor shots is as easy as pressing a button. No money wasted on defective film rolls!

- **Be patient.** Keep on clicking, and you're sure to produce some gems that will be a pleasure to look at for years to come.

## How to Make Your Kid "Fly," and Other Roughhousing Tips

Scientists have proven that physical play makes kids smart, physically fit, and socially aware. It's also a lot of fun—for your child and for you! It can be as simple as rolling in the grass or playing a game of tag. You're not in it to teach organized game rules; you're just out to have fun while engaging in safe exercise. Here's one way to give your child the experience of flying through the air, a perennial favorite among the little folks.

1. Find a wide open space and lie on your back.

2. Ask your child to stand by your feet.

3. Hold her hands and place your feet on her chest.

4. Bring your legs toward your chest; she will rise into the air, supported by your hands and feet.

5. Make airplane or rocket-ship noises as you gently rock back and forth and side to side.

6. Bring your child down for a safe landing by rolling her back to the starting position.

# How Not to Hurt Your Back

Your kid's having a great time, but *you* aren't a kid anymore, remember? When roughhousing with your children, it's important to be aware that your body isn't as limber as it once was, nor does it bounce back as easily. Before engaging in any type of extended horseplay, you should stretch your back, not to mention your neck and legs. If you've got a weak back in the first place, consider wearing a weightlifting belt. Also, be mindful of lifting and tossing your child, which, as he grows, eventually becomes the equivalent of throwing around a 40- to 60-pound weight.

## How to Build a Sand Castle

Building a seashore château is the perfect sun-and-surf family activity: it's creative, it's satisfying, it's free, and everyone can participate in the fun.

- **Gather and assess your tools.** You'll need a bucket or two in which to collect water and a shovel of some sort to move the sand. Though not necessary, cups or containers of varying sizes are ideal to give your castle an array of heights and shapes.

- **Have a loose plan.** Before getting down to building business, draw lines in the sand to identify the placement of the main castle, smaller towers, and walls as well as the moat and bridges (if you're feeling particularly ambitious). This outline will disappear as you start to build, but establishing a loose framework gives everyone a starting point and a goal to work toward, no matter how it ends up taking shape. (Note that some children—and adults—are happier improvising a creative vision rather than following a blueprint.)

*Make a plan and then start building!*

- **Build the main structure.** You can pile sand to form the main castle, creating a pyramid shape, or you can fill your largest bucket with wet sand and flip it over. (The consistency you want is not runny, goopy mud; it should be wet enough to stick together but dry enough to stay in place.) Be sure to pat the bottom of the bucket before gently lifting it up and away.

- **Construct the towers.** Fill a smaller bucket or a cup with wet sand and flip it over to create the towers.

- **Dig out the moat.** Using your hand or a shovel, remove the sand around the castle. Use the sand you dug out to form a wall with your hands.

- **Decorate.** Gather shells, pebbles, sticks, and seaweed to adorn your fortress.

- **Advanced options for older kids or show-off dads:** Bridges! Flags! Modern-day cities!

## The Birds and the Bees, Part 1: Where Do Babies Come From?

There's a pretty good chance your child will ask this question, and it's highly likely that the timing will catch you off guard. The important thing to remember is that she's asking out of real curiosity, so your response should be serious and thoughtful, however much or little you choose to say.

- **Ask your child what she already knows.** It's common for preschool-age children to talk about this topic, because many are welcoming a new baby into the family. It's important to hear what your child has heard or discerned from other conversations.

- **Consider your child's age.** Not only may the response for a toddler be different from that intended for a preschooler, but what the child is really asking may be different. A toddler may be curious about what's in Mommy's belly, whereas a preschooler may be more curious about how the baby got in, how the baby will get out, and how life will change when the new baby comes home.

- **Ask what your child imagines the answer might be.** In many cases, she may be able to answer her own question. Though she may not be exactly right, she might be close enough to satisfy her own curiosity, at least for the moment.

- **Consider how much you want to share.** Honesty is generally the best policy, especially in this case; there's never really a good reason to trot out the old line about the stork. Now, that doesn't mean you need to go into explicit detail. Answer the questions you are being asked. And let the follow-up questions dictate how much you need to share.

- **Consider your comfort level.** If you're uncomfortable speaking about this subject, simply say that you will explain it later. Meanwhile, feel free to consult an educator, a medical advisor, a religious advisor, and books and articles for tips and techniques for discussing the topic intelligently and appropriately.

# Big Kid Stuff

## How to Teach Your Child to Ride a Bicycle

Dad teaching child to ride a bike: It's a time-honored ritual filled with excitement, nerves, laughter, yelling, joy, frustration, and bruised egos. On both sides. No matter how bumpy the start, this milestone will bring an immense feeling of pride to you and a new sense of freedom to your child. Though the tools have changed, the basic principles remain the same. Off we go!

### Part 1: Training Wheels On

1. Purchase a bicycle equipped with training wheels and properly fitted to your child's height; store personnel will be able to help with sizes. Also, purchase a helmet and elbow and knee pads; unnecessary scrapes and bruises are, well, unnecessary, and it's best to start good habits right from the get-go.

2. Find a safe place to practice. A quiet sidewalk flanked with grass is ideal, but any flat secluded area will work fine.

Don't teach beginning bike skills on a road, no matter how infrequently traveled it may be.

3. Before beginning the lesson, teach your child to put on the helmet and pads. Take this opportunity to speak to him about the importance of wearing protective gear and biking in a safe and responsible manner. Also, explain that he might fall and that it's OK if he does.

4. Direct him to mount the bike in such a way that his feet remain on the ground. In other words, he may be standing and straddling the bike as opposed to sitting on the seat.

5. In this position, ask him to experiment with the handlebars by turning them left and right.

6. Next, direct him to sit on the seat and place his feet on the pedals. From this position, encourage him to lean left and right. Show him how to brake by pushing back on the pedals. Discuss the importance of knowing how to slow down and stop.

7. When he's ready, tell him to start pedaling. As he rides, ask him to turn, stop, and start to ensure that he has full control over the bicycle. Remind him to keep his eyes on the road in front of him, not on his feet.

## Part 2: Training Wheels Off

1. When you feel your child has control over the bicycle and is solidly balanced, you can discuss removing the training wheels. This process may take days, weeks, or even months. Just make sure you have a dialogue about his comfort level. It's all about building your child's self-confidence—there's no need to rush.

2. Remove the training wheels.

3. Have your child put on his helmet and protective padding.

4. Once again, find a flat secluded area.

5. Ask him to mount the bike so that his feet are on the ground. Have him push himself along in this position, "walking" the bike from atop the seat, so that he gets a feel for balance.

6. Ask him to start pedaling while you hold the back of the seat to keep it steady. You'll need to run alongside him while you do this.

7. When you feel he has achieved the proper balance and control, gently release the bike seat. Repeat several times. Offer encouraging words throughout, especially when he falls. (And fall he will. As you've already told him: it's OK. There's no other way to learn to ride a bike.)

## How to Encourage Outside Play

In today's world, video games, television, and the Internet provide an easy alternative to outside play. In moderation, those activities can positively impact your child's development. But they're no substitute for outdoor activities, which prepare young bodies and minds for a lifetime of physical and social health. Here are some ways to make sure the fun of being outside is more exciting and engaging than a day spent mesmerized in front of a video screen.

- **Provide a range of activities.** As always, by allowing your child to choose from several options, she'll feel more involved and enthusiastic about the idea of outdoor play. She may not be up for a trip to the playground swing set, but kicking a ball in the backyard just might sound like a blast.

- **Invite a friend.** "The more, the merrier" is oft repeated for a reason. Bringing along a playmate or two is usually a strong motivator for any type of activity.

- **Seek out community sports or activities.** Many townships and local clubs organize leagues that your child can join when old enough. Weekly practices and games will get kids outside on a regular basis.

- **Take up a hobby to do together.** Pick something that you and your child can do outside every weekend, say, a Saturday afternoon kite-flying expedition or a Sunday morning nature walk. Make it something special that only the two of you can share.

## Five Simple Tips on Nutrition

Most children are picky eaters. Many times, you'll be happy they're eating at all, never mind whether they're consuming the recommended daily dose of vitamins and minerals. But it's important to set your child on the path to a healthy life by building good habits of eating nutritional foods. Today we're bombarded with a wide and convenient array of unnecessarily fattening and high-sugar and salty foods. But good choices abound. Here instead are simple choices that will have substantial lifelong benefits.

- Choose skim or fat-free milk. When children are exposed to the flavor while young, they probably won't want the more fattening whole or two-percent milk later in life.

- Choose whole fruits or 100-percent fruit juice, which is typically lower in sugar.

- Choose cereals with low or no added sugar.

- Choose whole grain breads, which are higher in fiber.

- Choose to bake or roast your food instead of frying it.

## How to Host a Sleepover Party

Expect the first slumber-party requests to hit when your child is around eight years old. Start small by having one friend sleep over before you jump into the full-fledged sleeping-bag bash. And remember that although slumber parties are traditionally portrayed in our culture as a "girl thing," that's not really an accurate reflection of reality. Boys love sleepovers, too. Here are a few tips for containing the festivities to a modicum of mayhem.

1. If possible, send younger siblings over to Grandma's for the night. Not only will it mean fewer children for you to worry about, it will keep the siblings from feeling left out.

2. Arrange for the guests to arrive right before dinner.

3. Plan an activity to keep the kids busy while you prepare dinner: a scavenger hunt in the backyard, a craft project, or, heck, include the kids in preparing dinner! Try picking up some pizza dough from your grocer's prepared foods section and

*Keep the party going all night long—*
*or at least until bedtime.*

    let the kids add the sauce and toppings.

4. Skip dessert at the table and tell the children to change into their pajamas.

5. The ideal evening activity is a movie served up with special-occasion treats (popcorn, ice cream sundaes, s'mores, etc.).

6. Make sure you've selected a film that's age appropriate. A scary movie is not a good idea until the kids are in junior high.

7. After the movie, some kids may be ready for bed. Suggest that the others play a board game or talk quietly.

8. Use your judgment to decide when you should enforce bedtime for everyone.

9. In the morning, a dad who's feeling particularly ambitious (and savvy in the kitchen) might serve up pancakes or French toast. But most kids will be perfectly happy with something simpler: bagels, cereal, etc.

10. Encourage the kids to play until their parents arrive to pick them up.

## Five Great Jokes to Make Your Child Giggle

**Q:** Why was the baby ant confused?
**A:** Because all of its uncles were ants.

**Q:** What do you get when you mix SpongeBob SquarePants with Albert Einstein?
**A:** SpongeBob SmartyPants!

**Q:** Why is Cinderella bad at sports?
**A:** Because she has a pumpkin for a coach and she runs away from the ball.

**Q:** Why is 6 afraid of 7?
**A:** Because 7 8 9!

*And, finally, this oldie but goodie. You may have heard it a million times, but your child never has!*

**You:** Knock-knock.
**Kid:** Who's there?
**You:** Banana.
**Kid:** Banana who?
**You:** Knock-knock.

**Kid:** Who's there?
**You:** Banana.
**Kid:** Banana who?
**You:** Knock-knock.
**Kid:** Who's there?
**You:** Orange.
**Kid:** Orange who?
**You:** Orange you glad I didn't say banana?

## How to Keep a Family Happy During Car Trips

"Don't make me turn this car around."
—Every dad who's ever lived

When that idle threat doesn't work, here are some ideas for keeping everybody (relatively) happy during that drive to Grandma's house (or anyplace that involves being in a car long enough for a young mind to get bored sitting still).

- **Plan ahead.** If the trip will be long, identify places to stop along the way: restaurants, coffee shops, roadside attractions, a playground, etc.

- **Play a game.** Classic car games, like I Spy, the License Plate Game, and 20 Questions, keep your child thinking and engaged with the outside world. (Just make sure that, if you too are going to play, you don't miss a turn while trying to decide if Oscar the Grouch is an animal, vegetable, or mineral.)

- **Play music.** Take turns selecting songs. To make it interesting, give passengers the power to veto one selection, allowing them to skip a tune they just don't like. Alternatively, prepare a playlist featuring a mix of each person's favorites.

- **Plan a window scavenger hunt.** Before the trip, give each passenger a list of things to spot during the drive. Then take turns calling out the items as they're spotted.

- **Play a video game or watch a movie.** Yes, if your children are old enough, portable DVD players and handheld video game devices will keep them quiet for hours. Just don't let them overstrain their eyes.

- **Pack snacks.** Break out the nibbles at strategic times. Aim for foods that are safe to eat in a car and easy to clean off upholstery.

## How to Support Your Child's Successes and Failures

Naturally, you want your child to excel in everything. And, just as obviously, nobody is good at everything. There will almost certainly be plenty of successes and failures to celebrate along the way, and knowing how to support your child in either situation is important.

- **Pay attention in the first place.** If it's a sport or competition, volunteer to coach or simply be on the sidelines cheering from the stands. If the activity takes place at school, attend parent-teacher conferences. You can't be properly supportive if you don't know what's going on.

- **Assess the situation.** If your child is underperforming, it's often tempting to blame a teacher or coach rather than accept that your child needs help. Review the facts and keep an open mind. Should it turn out that there really is an issue with an adult in authority, approach the person's superior to calmly discuss the problem and reach a solution.

- **Have a conversation.** After any kind of performance—whether a report card, sports match, stage production, whatever—talk with your child about it. Be sure to praise a job well done. If your child needs improvement in a particular area, discuss the whys and hows and what needs to happen to improve. And remember to distinguish between your child's serious work and optional time-filling activities; the latter should be fun, not a source of psychological pressure.

- **Work together.** Spend some time together on the field or at the table addressing the areas you discussed. Your participation and investment of time and energy show that it's important to you.

- **Recognize achievements and milestones.** Whether it's continued success or an incremental improvement, acknowledge it.

## The Truth about Cats and Dogs

Welcoming a pet into the family can be a positive experience for everyone. Learning to care for an animal can teach your children responsibility and help them develop social skills. But having a pet also comes with the need to care for that pet. Remember these important points.

- **Be realistic.** Despite promises and protestations, YOU will be responsible for the pet's care. Children will say anything to get that dog or cat or gerbil or tarantula. They may even mean it. But pets, like children, require 24-hour care, and an 11-year-old will probably not wake up at midnight to walk a sick dog.

- **Plan for additional expenses.** Pets are expensive. They require training. They eat. They visit the doctor and need medicine. They may even require surgery. Sounds a lot like children, no? Be sure to consider all the financial commitments that come with adding this nonhuman member to your household.

- **Have travel contingency plans.** Pets cannot be left alone for long periods. If your family likes to travel, you'll need to be comfortable with the idea of hiring a pet-sitter or paying for boarding in a kennel.

- **Be ready to make a long-term commitment.** Dogs and cats can live 10 to 15 years; horses for twice that long. Your 11-year-old daughter may have graduated from college and you'll still be caring for her childhood pet.

- **With great responsibility comes great joy.** Pets are loving, loyal, and a lot of fun. The fun times ought to outweigh the headaches by far. If you're comfortable with the responsibility, then adopting a pet is a wonderful thing to do. But, first, spend plenty of time discussing and researching the type of animal that's right for your family: dog vs. cat vs. horse vs. gerbil vs. goldfish; bouncy puppy or kitten vs. mature, sedate, well-trained house pet.

# When a Pet Dies

Over time, your child will come to view your pet as a member of the family—a furry (or scaly or whatever) sibling who welcomes them home, plays with them, cuddles up close. They will develop a special bond. And, unfortunately, this great joy brings with it the sadness of saying good-bye. You cannot shelter your child from this sadness and pain—and you shouldn't, for this is how they learn about life—but you can help them cope with it. Here are a few suggestions for easing the grief of losing a dear animal friend.

- Share the news in a way that is appropriate for your child's age. Use discretion when deciding how much to share. If possible, tell your child one-on-one and at home.

- If you have to euthanize your pet, first explain that the veterinarian did everything possible to prolong your pet's life. Avoid the words "put to sleep" or "going to sleep," since your child may take these literally. If your child is old enough, he may want to say good-bye.

- If your pet dies suddenly, explain briefly what occurred and let your child's questions guide the discussion. Again, share as much or as little as you feel comfortable with, but be truthful in your responses.

- You and your child will likely experience a similar range of emotions. You don't need to hide them. If you're moved to cry, go ahead. Expressing your emotions and talking about your feelings will set an example and may help your child share his own feelings and cope with the situation.

- After the initial shock fades, you will want to help your child heal. You may want to hold a ceremonial burial for your pet to provide a sense of closure. Share stories and memories of your pet. Speak to your child and let him know that his sadness will pass, but the memories will last forever.

# The Birds and the Bees, Part 2: Awkward Questions About Grown-Up Relationships

Guess what? Your child is human, and humans are inherently interested in sex. Questions will inevitably come up. You may stumble a bit as you grasp for the right word or phrase, but a little preparation can ease the stress and make for a productive conversation.

- **Address the question when it's asked.** If, however, you're in a public setting where it seems inappropriate to discuss such matters, explain that you'll talk about the subject when you get home so that you can discuss it fully and without distractions.

- **Respond with a few questions of your own.** A gentle "What prompted you to ask this now?" can help you gain perspective and may even point to the answer. "What do you think?" will help you get a sense of what she may already know—right or wrong.

- **Use the proper terms for body parts.** And state them matter-of-factly. Any awkwardness that some people may experience from words like *penis* and *vagina* typically occurs because these words have been presented as "dirty" or "secret." By using them in a straight, factual manner, you're teaching your child that it's OK to use them and to acknowledge what they refer to.

- **Answer honestly.** As stated many times throughout this book, it is important to answer questions truthfully. At this specific age, your child may be talking with friends about sex. It's important that you help her separate fact from fiction and not add to the confusion.

## How to Assign Chores

Every household comes with myriad tasks, and, let's be honest, you'd love to unload a few of them. Sure, the short-term benefit is getting some help around the house. But the long-term benefit is that it teaches children responsibility to themselves and to others.

- **Start young, and start small.** Younger children can be taught how to make their beds and clean up their toys after playtime. Older children can set the dinner table and put away laundry. Preteens and teenagers can tackle larger responsibilities, like taking out the garbage, grocery shopping, and raking the leaves.

- **Teach your child how to properly perform the chore.** No matter what age or what chore, it is important to be clear about the correct way to achieve the desired result. Demonstrate the task several times, and do it with them the first few times.

- **Show your appreciation.** Give them time to learn and provide feedback and compliments.

- **Don't assign chores based on out-moded gender roles.** Your son will need to know how to cook and clean. Your daughter will need to know how to rake and mow the lawn.

- **Older kids should be paid an allow-ance for doing household chores.** Being paid for their work teaches children the value of money, and it demonstrates that rewards come for a job well done. Younger children may not be ready to fully grasp this lesson, but you can still reward them by tracking their work, using stickers on a chart prominently displayed.

## How to Interact with Your Child's Teachers

Your child's success at school will benefit enormously from your involvement. Make time to forge relationships with his teachers as well as the school's administration.

- **Attend (and participate in) activities.** Whether it's an open house or a parent-teacher conference, take a moment to introduce yourself (and your child, when necessary and appropriate). Use this time to bring up special needs or circumstances of your child's education. Also, ask teachers about their preferred method of communication: face-to-face meetings, telephone, e-mail, etc.

- **Respect the teacher's time.** If you want to arrange a meeting, defer to the teacher's schedule. If you bump into each other outside of school, don't jump on that off-hours opportunity to discuss your child's education.

- **Be polite.** You are, correctly, possessive and protective of your child. Therefore, when speaking with teachers, avoid making assertions, such as "You should" or "You need to." Instead, listen carefully to the teacher's perspective before sharing your own. Keep the teacher's concerns in mind while politely offering your own ideas or suggestions.

- **Accept the response.** Although you may disagree with your child's teachers, you shouldn't argue with them (but, if you must, certainly do *not* do so in front of your child). A contentious relationship can lead to a downward spiral of bad feelings that may end up dumped on your child's shoulders. In minor matters, accept the teacher's authority and find ways to help your child handle it. If major disagreements about your child's education remain unresolved, calmly take the discussion to the principal.

- **Discuss progress regularly.** Gauge improvement often by following up with both child and teacher.

## How to Arm Your Child against Peer Pressure

Peer pressure is all around us. Even as adults we feel the desire to be liked, and sometimes it's tempting to avoid interpersonal conflict by ignoring our better judgment and going along with the crowd. But standing up for ourselves in the face of other people's behavior is all about making the right choices—choices we're proud of. Your job as a dad is to make sure your child has the self-confidence to make her own choices and take responsibility for them.

- **Don't be shy.** Have an open discussion with your child about her feelings on sex, drugs, alcohol, and other issues where peer pressure may come into play.

- **Discuss in advance how to respond to peer pressure.** A scripted, rehearsed response for certain predictable types of situations can help save your child from being taken by surprise and stammering out the "Uh . . . OK" that tends to fill awkward moments.

- **Speak to her about leadership, trust, and responsibility.** Main points: She will be responsible for the outcomes of her choices. You trust her to make the appropriate decisions. She should feel comfortable asserting her individualism in situations where everyone else is doing something she's uncomfortable with.

- **Stay in the loop.** Check in regularly to learn what's going on with her friends and at school. Speak to other parents. To understand your child, you need a solid understanding of the world she faces every day.

Teen Stuff
and Beyond

## How to Speak to Your Child About Drugs and Alcohol

It used to be so much simpler, right? How'd we go from bike rides and sand castles to sex, drugs, and alcohol? Well, kids grow up quickly, and today's media-saturated world exposes them to a lot of things at an earlier age than we might remember from our own childhoods. As a dad, it's your job to prepare your child before problems arise, arming her with sound advice so she's equipped to make the right decisions.

- **Pick your child's brain.** Find out what she knows about drugs and alcohol and if she's already been exposed to or experimented with them.

- **Discuss the effects of alcohol and drug usage.** Speak to your child about the short- and long-term effects on both body and mind. Make sure she understands the dangers of driving under the influence. (You'll probably want to confirm that her school's health or driver's education class is showing those horrible but effective educational films with the pictures of dead teenagers.)

- **Establish a clear family position based on the underlying laws.** Drugs are illegal. So is alcohol until your child is 21. (You may, however, want to allow ceremonial glasses of weak wine at family holiday dinners, so that your child doesn't glamorize the taboo of drinking but understands that it is often just a regular part of adult life.)

- **Acknowledge the pressure she may be under to experiment.** Make it clear that she has a choice and you trust her to make the right decision. Role-play various scenarios so that she has practice saying "no."

- **Check in periodically.** If you suspect a problem, seek professional advice privately from a substance-abuse counselor who specializes in teenagers.

## How to Teach Your Child to Drive

Hire an instructor. Seriously. You entrust your children to professionals for so many other facets of their education, why stop here? But if, like so many dads, you're certain you and only you are the best person to teach your child to drive, follow these steps.

1. Take a field trip with your child to your local DMV to pick up a driver's training manual. This booklet is full of important information, including traffic laws, procedures, and safety tips. It's imperative for your child to master this information, particularly the signs and limitations. This trip should happen well ahead of any hands-on training to allow your child time to read, digest, and memorize. (Pop quizzing—pun intended—is always a good way to help internalize new learning, and that's especially true with driver's ed, since surprise questions resemble the unexpected situations a driver faces on the road.)

2. After your child receives a learner's permit, let him sit behind the wheel of a parked car. Adjust the seat and steering wheel so he can comfortably reach the wheel and pedals. Show him the proper hand positions on the wheel (10 and 2 o'clock). Adjust the mirrors, and discuss the importance of using mirrors to monitor your position in relation to other cars.

3. Help your child get comfortable with the vehicle's controls. Point out the ignition, gear shift, and emergency break as well as the controls for turn signals, wipers, and hazard and headlights. Explain their functions. Practice using the turn signals. Don't forget to show where the insurance and registration are stored.

4. Drive to a remote place—preferably a large, empty parking lot—to practice. Along the way, explain the what, why, and how of some of the less obvious actions you're taking as you drive, like using mirrors to guide you while changing lanes and braking well in advance of a stop sign or red light. When you reach

your practice location, use cones or chalk to mark a route, including lanes. Indicate locations of stop signs.

5. Switch spots, letting your child sit behind the wheel. Relax. Remind yourself to be patient. Take slow deep breaths. Did I mention you should stay calm? Fasten your safety belt and remind your child, one more time, that everyone in a car he's driving should always be buckled in.

6. Tell your child to start the car. Direct him to drive forward along the marked route. Make sure he's driving at an appropriate speed, staying in his lane, and stopping completely at the stop sign, not rolling past or through it.

7. Practice changing lanes. Be sure that your child uses the turn signal and mirrors. Instruct him to look quickly over his shoulder before changing lanes because the mirror may have a blind spot. (Note: For practice, you could equip the car's side mirrors with adhesive blind-spot mirrors, which are inexpensive and take only a minute to mount.)

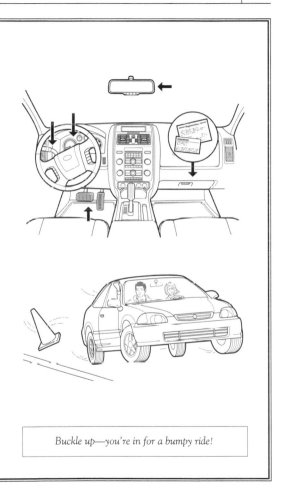

*Buckle up—you're in for a bumpy ride!*

8. Next, let your child practice driving in reverse. Direct him to back up to a certain point. Be sure he uses his mirrors and looks over his shoulder. Confirm aloud that he has stopped at the appropriate spot.

9. Last, do some practice parking. (At this point, teach head-in parking only. You can introduce parallel parking later, after your child has mastered the other skills described above.)

10. Take time to practice all the above steps, and do so as many times as necessary. Be patient—there's no rush. Address oversights as they arise, and praise good behavior.

11. When you feel your child is ready, introduce road driving. Start with a quiet neighborhood, which will allow him to drive at a slower speed and with fewer distractions. Let him get comfortable using the brakes to stop at stop signs and turn signals throughout the neighborhood. Remind him to stay to the right of the road, even in small one-lane streets.

12. When your child has proved he's comfortable with small-street driving, advance to slightly busier streets. This will allow him to grow accustomed to more cars both in front and behind traveling at greater speeds. It will also teach him to deal with oncoming traffic. Caveat. This experience is likely to be tense for both of you. Remind your child—and yourself—to stay calm and focused.

13. When you're both feeling comfortable—ideally, after a few weeks of practice on local roads—it's time to take it to the highways, freeways, and interstates. Reinforce all the elements learned in the earlier stages, for now they'll come into play in a new environment. Remind your child that the ramps and entry lanes are used to increase your speed to match the flow of traffic. (By contrast, when approaching exit ramps, it's necessary to slow to their posted speeds.) He should drive for a while in the right lane—acclimating himself to this new situation—before he practices passing and changing lines.

14. Continue to remind your child about the importance of safety: no goofing around while driving with friends, absolutely no cell phones or texting behind the wheel, and—of course—no driving after drinking. Ever.

# How to Handle Your Child's First Car Accident or Ticket

Congratulations! Your child has a driver's license. Well, the good news is that you no longer have to play chauffeur all around town. The bad news is that you now live with the added stress of knowing that your child is operating a motor vehicle. No matter how well you taught her and no matter how well she drives, accidents and speeding tickets are part and parcel of life behind the wheel. Here's what to do when confronted with this bump in the road.

- **Relax.** Stay calm. Assuming that everyone is unharmed, then everything else is able to be fixed and set to right.

- **Listen.** Ask your child to explain what happened. You'll probably sense that she's as upset as you are about the situation. Reassure her that you'll always be there when something goes wrong.

- **Remind her of the importance of safety.** Whether she was speeding or involved in an accident, use this event as a learning experience. Explain the consequences that moving violations have on her driving record and how they negatively impact insurance premiums.

- **Get her back on the road.** This step is particularly important if she was in an accident, for she may be reluctant to drive again right away. Don't push, but don't coddle either. Simply take the time to shepherd her through the anxiety before it saps her self-confidence.

# The Birds and the Bees, Part 3: Puberty and Sexual Behavior

By the time your child reaches the teenage years, the two of you should have already had several conversations about sex. There's no such thing as "the talk"; as you've read in this book, the dialogue is ongoing and starts as early as curiosity dictates. As adolescence gets under way, your child may be newly curious about experimentation and may have already started discussing things with friends. At this point, it's a good idea to restart the exchange and discuss sexual behavior frankly and openly.

- **Ask leading questions.** Starting with openers such as "Do you have any questions about sex?" and "Are your friends talking about sex?" will give you perspective on what your child already knows—or thinks he knows.

- **Explain sex.** There's a *lot* of information easily available today, so your child has probably picked up plenty already. Just make sure he's got it right. Be clear that sex is a bond between two adults who care deeply about the other's well-being. Be sure to find out if your child understands what he's heard about all types of sexual activity, not just the mechanics of reproduction.

- **Reinforce key elements:**

  - *Everyone has a choice.* He's the only one who can know for sure if and when he's adult enough to take this step. He should not succumb to pressure from his friends or partner. Remind him that there's nothing wrong with choosing to abstain from sex until he's met the person he wants to spend the rest of his life with.

  - *It's important to respect other people's choices.* Sex should never be forced, cajoled, or manipulated. It should happen only when both people are truly eager and ready for intimacy.

  - *Flying solo is fine.* Sure, it's awkward to discuss masturbation with your child. But it's more important to be certain he's got the message that, until he's ready for an adult relationship, it's safer and smarter to take care of his own sexual urges than to rush into a premature union.

- *Practice safe sex*. Discuss the purposes of condoms and birth control. Discuss the possible life-changing ramifications of unprotected sex, including pregnancy and sexually transmitted diseases.

- **Seek out other resources.** You and your child should consult medical professionals, guidance counselors, spiritual leaders, and/or other books to learn the best options for approaching and discussing the subject of sex. The key is to remember that your child will be curious—just as you were—and needs wise advice to successfully navigate all the information and misinformation that's out there concerning sexual activity.

## Five Great Activities That Allow You to Bond with Your Teen

Think back to when you were a teenager. In all likelihood, you were far more preoccupied with your friends, the opposite sex, and the newfound freedom of driving a car than you were with spending your leisure time with family. As a dad, however, you'll soon realize how important it is to stay connected to your teenager.

- **Eat dinner together.** Work, school, and activity schedules can be hectic. But everyone has to eat, right? Prioritize a sit-down meal together as often as you can. It makes for an easy, natural time to check in.

- **Plan a movie or game night.** A night at home is easy and safe. And be sure to let your child pick the movie or game.

- **Share a hobby.** Fix a car. Take golf lessons. Plant a garden. Take a dance class. Learn to sail. Choose something that interests you both. Finding common ground can lead to a lifetime of memories.

- **Plan a trip.** Maybe it's an extended road trip, or it could be a weekend spent camping in the woods. Involve your child in every stage of the planning, from scheduling and choosing the mode of transportation to choosing activities and shopping for meals.

- **Volunteer for a charity.** Either make a regular donation of time or sign up for an annual charity event, like a walk-a-thon or bike race, where participants raise money for a cause you all believe in. The result is quality time spent together, all while teaching your child the importance of community service.

## Privacy: How Much Is Enough?

It's natural for any teenager to want time alone. Privacy is incredibly important to us all, especially teens. Kids spend a lot of time interacting with the world—in school, during extracurricular activities, on sports teams, and at home. What's more, as a teen your child has reached the age where she has the increased freedom to explore more on her own. She needs space to internalize her world and have private conversations with friends about things ranging from school and romantic relationships to simple entertainment and silliness.

The amount of privacy you provide is directly related to how much you trust your child. And that trust is created through your ongoing relationship. It's important to respect your child's mood swings and bad days, but it's equally important to find time to connect and discuss what she's doing and where she's going and to reinforce the house rules. After all, you are the parent.

## How to Select a College

Choosing any school—pre-K, elementary, secondary, and beyond—can be overwhelming. At the higher-education level, it's even more so. Not only are there tons of institutions to choose from, it's also a sizable investment in your child's future. Consider the following points before you decide.

- **Assess the programs offered and degrees conferred.** If your child is certain about the field she wants to pursue, you'll need to find a school that offers that program. If she's unsure, look for a school with a broad range of programs.

- **Consider location.** If your child wants to stay closer to home, that factor will drive your search. Other concerns to bear in mind: urban, suburban, or country setting; noisy or quiet campus; cozy and contained or supersize and sprawling? Discuss your child's preferences before even filling out an application.

- **Contemplate the costs.** Tuition rates vary and will increase every year your child is enrolled. Additional out-of-pocket expenses to figure into your budget include room and board, travel, and extracurricular activities. Be sure to do the math to gauge what you can realistically afford.

- **Size matters.** Larger institutions usually offer a broader range of programs and activities, whereas smaller ones tend to tout their reduced class sizes and more personal attention. It's important to understand your child's learning style and match her to an appropriate average class size.

- **Research some more.** Once you and your child have narrowed your search to a handful of schools, look into the reputation and rankings of each. Visit all the schools personally, if possible, and take an official tour. While there, talk to students and faculty.

- **Don't be persuaded by others.** Selecting a college should not be based solely on family legacy or a boyfriend's/girlfriend's choice. Your child must make the decision that best suits his or her own life and goals.

## How to Give Advice without Seeming Pushy

As a teenager, your child faces many new situations and challenges. He'll also want to assert his independence and assure you that he knows what he's doing. During these times, it may be difficult for you to bite your tongue and withhold criticism and advice. But although your child may not actively seek out your advice, he may be more receptive to it than first appears. You just need to present it in the proper way.

• **Keep it conversational.** Don't open with, "We need to talk." Nobody likes the sound of that, including you. Introduce the topic as part of another conversation, casually, so it almost seems tangential.

• **Don't be critical.** Offer advice by spinning it from the negative to the positive. Also, praise what he's doing well before you counsel him on ways to make it better.

• **Make it sound like it's his idea.** Ask questions that will lead him to the answer. When he stumbles upon your solution, commend him for his great idea and encourage him to try it.

## How to Meet the Love of Your Child's Life

Whether it's the first boyfriend or the fiancée, this moment can be stressful and emotional for you and your wife. The key to making the encounter easy is to prepare ahead, ready to deflect those unexpected uncomfortable moments.

- **Find out his or her name beforehand.** Commit it to memory.

- **Ask to see a picture.** Checking out a recent photo will help you avoid an awkward initial reaction.

- **Find out a little bit about him or her.** If you're planning to serve a meal, learn the types of food he or she prefers or avoids. To ensure a smooth flow of conversation, be sure to ask your child about the significant other's interests, line of work, or leisurely pursuits and hobbies.

- **Keep it casual.** The chatter should be light. The setting should be easy and manageable. And it's OK to keep the first meeting short.

- **Keep your opinion to yourself.** There's no need to argue with your child or, even worse, your child's date. Save your opinions for later. If you have concerns, consider the most appropriate way to voice them to your child.

*Remember: Never jump to judgment.*

## How to Meet Your Child's In-Laws

As hard as it may be to imagine now, that day will probably come. Once married, your child will add a whole new group of people to the family tree. The closeness of the relationship depends on how interested both sides are in having a relationship. Regardless of how friendly you end up being, it's imperative to maintain a cordial rapport with your child's in-laws, who are sure to be a big part of your child's life. Here's how to start things off right.

- **Be courteous and involved in the conversation.** Ask about their background. Share yours. Get to know one another.

- **Don't make it a competition.** They may have a nicer house than you. You may take more exotic vacations. They may have certain ways of celebrating holidays. You may live closer to the kids. It's all good. Don't measure yourselves against one another.

- **Be open to sharing.** Your child now has two sets of parents to spend time with.

Most likely, time will need to be split with the in-laws. Be respectful of that. Don't turn it into a debate, neither with your child nor with the in-laws.

- **Do what's best for the kids—always.** Remember why it is that you're meeting: for the happiness of your children. Use that principle to guide you throughout your relationship with the in-laws.

## Stuff You Should Know That I Can't Tell You

Your child's birthday

Your child's middle name

Your child's religious name

Your child's favorite food

Your child's favorite color

Your child's best friend

Your child's school (name, location) and teacher's name

Your child's hobbies

Your child's allergies

Your child's pediatrician (name and contact information)

The location of the nearest emergency room

## Acknowledgments

A sincere thanks to everyone at Quirk Books for making this and every book we publish great. Thanks to Randi, Ilivia, and Sawyer. Thanks to Phil, Sheryl, Harvey, Rosalie, Lena, Mandi, Adam, Lexi, Brett, Shawn, Andrew, Ashley, Hailey, Brian, Pamela, and Teddy. Thanks to Adam, Brad, Bieb, Dave, Jason, Jay, Jeff, Joe, Josh, Matt, Matzner, Michael, Scott, SOHK, and CORE.

And a hearty thanks to dads everywhere!

**Also available:**

Stuff Every Man
Should Know

Recipes Every Man
Should Know

facebook.com/stuffmenshouldknow